YOGA IN THE KASHMIR TRADITION

THE ART OF LISTENING

FOLLOWING THE TEACHINGS OF JEAN KLEIN

y

BILLY DOYLE

NON-DUALITY PRESS

YOGA IN THE KASHMIR TRADITION

First edition published October 2014 by NON-DUALITY PRESS

© Billy Doyle 2014
© Non-Duality Press 2014

Billy Doyle has asserted his right under the Copyright, Designs and Patents Act, 1988, to be identified as author of this work.

All rights reserved
No part of this book may be reproduced or utilised in any form or by any means, electronic or mechanical, without prior permission in writing from the Publisher.

NON-DUALITY PRESS | PO Box 2228 | Salisbury | SP2 2GZ
United Kingdom

ISBN: 978-1-908664-41-9

www.non-dualitypress.org

in gratitude

to Jean Klein,

my teacher

It is important to live this directionlessness, this not-knowing, this waiting without waiting for anything. It acts on your cells, on your psychosomatic body, bringing them to dilation and harmony. All that remains is your directionless awareness. Live in this absolute absence of yourself. It is the threshold. You are in complete openness, open to nothing, free from all ideas, free from all hope. And when you are completely transparent, open to openness, you are taken by Truth, by Grace. That is certain.

Jean Klein, *The Book of Listening*

CONTENTS

Introduction xi
Advaita Vedanta 1
The Art of Listening 5
Listening to the Body 7
The Process of Letting Go 13
Giving Weight to the Ground: *Shavasana* 17
    Tensing—releasing 19
    Lifting—dropping 20
    Lifting—placing 20
    Letting go with each exhalation 21
Letting the Sensation Unfold 23
The Opening of the Senses 29
    The mouth 30
    The ears 32
    The skin 34
    The nostrils 36
    The eyes 37
    Eye exercises 40

Healing with colour 42

The brain 43

What We Take in 45

Discovering our Verticality: Right Sitting 47

The Breath—Letting it Flow 53

The space between each breath 54

Exploring our capacity to breathe: sensing it
in different parts 56

Taking charge of the breath: expanding
the breath 58

Whole body as breath 59

The expansion of the breath in space 60

The breath and verticality 61

Healing with the breath 62

Pranayama: *Nadi Shodhana*, Alternate Nostril Breathing... 63

Other sequences 66

The breath as a pointer to the ultimate 67

Expanding in the Space 69

Bring space to your body 71

Bring space to your joints 72

Letting your bones float away 73

From one healthy part: letting the feeling spread 74

From Being to Sensation to Movement 77
       Raising arms.. 80
Working with the Energy Body 84
Paschimottanasana: Sitting Forward Bend 87
Ardha Matsyendrasana: Half Spinal Twist 95
Trikonasana: Triangle 99
Meditation 105
Guided Meditation 114

Quotations from *Vijnana Bhairava* 117
Recommended Books 119

INTRODUCTION

Yoga in the Kashmir Tradition presents yoga as I experienced it working with Jean Klein. Jean brought this approach to the West in the 1950s and during subsequent years he further developed and refined the teaching.

Jean Klein was a master of Advaita Vedanta (non-duality) in the tradition of Ramana Maharshi and Shri Atmananda Krishna Menon; however, he had his own distinctive and unique approach.

I first met Jean in 1982 when he was giving a series of discourses in London. I was deeply affected by his talk and afterwards he mentioned that he also taught yoga in his retreats. Being a yoga teacher myself, I was intrigued that he should also teach body work.

He was to become my teacher and for the following fourteen years I attended his retreats and talks in Holland, England, France and the USA as well as receiving private tuition. The retreats consisted of dialogues, question and answers, silent and guided meditation and the practices of yoga. He called this approach to body work, 'Yoga in the Kashmir Tradition'.

Here I will be focusing on his teachings regarding yoga, but as the whole sphere of his approach, be it self-enquiry, meditation or body work, was totally integrated, so these different aspects are intertwined through the book.

Jean had studied medicine and was a musicologist. In 1954 he left France and went to India for three years; it was at Bangalore University where he was studying that Jean met his guru, Pandiji, who was a professor of Sanskrit. His yoga teacher was Krishnamacharya of Madras, but whilst Jean was living in Bangalore he also met a yogi, Dibianandapuri, who had lived a long time in Kashmir. It was Dibianandapuri who introduced Jean to the Kashmir teachings and confirmed his understanding that the real body was the energy body and not the physical body. He showed him how all the yoga postures could be carried out on the subtle level independently of the physical body.

The nature of Jean's teaching when he returned to Europe was focused on the questions: *What is our real nature? Who am I?* Yoga was part of this enquiry. Even before his visit to India, Jean had a particular interest in the relationship between body function and psychology. Most teachers tend either to stress self-enquiry to the exclusion of body work or focus on body work with little regard for self-enquiry, but with Jean there was a marriage of approaches.

Jean explains in the following two paragraphs why the body work is important:

> *About a year after I returned from India I found it necessary to expand the teaching to the psychosomatic level. It became apparent, through meeting people, that*

> *identification with what we are not is confirmed and reinforced by contraction on the psychosomatic level. The I-concept is only a contraction on the level of the body-mind. It has no more reality than a bad habit. It is a defence against being nobody.*
>
> *In getting to know the body-mind, one can discover more clearly the nature of identification, and so let it go. The relaxed body is a relaxed mind. In a relaxed body and mind you are open to receiving, available, welcoming, open to the openness. The relaxed, light, energetic, sattvic body-mind is a near expression of our real nature. It is almost impossible for a conditioned body-mind to be receptive to truth, open to grace. It can happen that truth pierces through all conditioning, since the insight into our true nature ultimately has nothing to do with the body or the mind. But it is exceedingly rare. My teaching also on the level of the body was only to make discrimination more likely, to help more of my friends be available to global insight.*
>
> Jean Klein, *Transmission of the Flame*

We might say, and understand theoretically, that we are not the body, senses and mind since they are simply objects in awareness. But do we really know what this body is? It is the contraction and defences on the level of the body that reinforce our identification with a particular body-mind. The body is in many ways an intricate defence mechanism which maintains our self-image. It is only by exploring the body that we free it from its habitual patterns and discover the real body. This exploration is the art of listening; of course this listening is not restricted to the ears—all the senses are involved and receptive. In freeing the body from restriction and coming to the expanded body, we have a fore-feeling of our real nature, our globality. The understanding of our real nature takes place on every level of our being, even the cells of our body are affected in the transformation—otherwise the transformation remains partial.

ADVAITA VEDANTA

At the core of the great religious traditions there is the understanding of the oneness of the whole of life. In the Indian tradition this is known as advaita, which means 'not two'. This truth lies at the heart of the Upanishads, and was later expounded by Sri Shankaracarya in the ninth century. Indeed, this is a current running through the whole of Indian culture.

Advaita asks us to question what is real, to question the common-sense view that we are separate entities, each body-mind being distinct from other body-minds and from the world. It asks: *What is our essential nature?* The body and mind are always changing. Is there not something that is beyond the flux of time? Is there not something beyond the mind? To recognise change there must be something in us that is changeless. What is changeless in me? Is it not the sense of presence, the sense of knowing? I know myself, I know the world, but the real question is: *Who is the knower?*

We don't cease to be when there is no thought; we still know that we are, but we generally only know ourselves in relation to objects, such as thoughts, images, memory. In other words, I am a woman, I am a doctor, I'm young, a person of worth. We don't know ourselves without the adornment of a string of characteristics.

It is this identification with an I-image, which is no more than a projection of the mind, that veils our true reality. Taking myself to be a limited separate entity in a universe invites fear and desire. In fact, fear and desire are the very essence of this separate personal entity. It is from this state of insecurity that we begin to look for happiness, for security. In the beginning this search is usually directed towards material objects, acquiring knowledge, enhancing our self-image, or towards relationships. Only when we realise from our failures that nothing in the world will completely satisfy our longing, do we begin to ask deeper questions.

This is the beginning of a more conscious spiritual search. We begin to realise what we are not: not a body, not a personality, not a series of images, not any kind of object. Our real nature is prior to any image, any thought. The body is in awareness, the mind is in awareness, the world too exists in awareness. Thus, awareness is prior to all manifestation.

We begin to give precedence to awareness and not to what we're aware of. We begin to feel ourselves as awareness, a witness to the passing show. Like the screen in the film show, the images are always changing, but the screen is unaffected. A feeling of space opens up between what I am and what I'm aware of. I begin to feel my autonomy, that I'm free of all things. I'm no longer locked in space and time, rather space and time are in me.

We come to understand, and actually *feel*, that consciousness is non-localised, that all that is perceived is in consciousness. There is not a separate seer and an object seen. The seen is in the seeing; there is no seen without the seeing. All that is perceived is of the very nature of consciousness. Here we stand in freedom, no longer an inside or outside, a separate me and a separate you. All is an expression of love, all is love. All is God, there is nothing but God.

The separate 'I' of the mind dissolves with this understanding. Life carries on, but without the burden of being somebody there is real functioning, not from a centre, but from love. It is not that I become something other, it is simply the recognition of what I always am, free of the illusion of being some separate entity. It is not that I progress through various spiritual levels, rather there is an ever deepening seeing that this 'me' that I have taken myself to be has no reality. Enlightenment is not *of* somebody, but freedom from *being* somebody.

> *When you proceed from the relative to the ultimate in stages your ego remains engaged. There is end-gaining. You are bound to the object. You may undo earlier conditioning but you merely learn a new conditioning, often one that is less flexible and interesting! When even the slightest emphasis is put on attaining, you continue the habit of objectifying your freedom and joy. You still say, 'I have experienced this.' You are still doing something. You remain in fraction. You take yourself for a prisoner with the goal of freedom. But the premise itself is an illusion. There is nothing to gain, and nothing to lose.*
>
> Jean Klein, *Who Am I?*

From the beginning, Jean stressed the importance of being open to the possibility that our real nature is timeless, spaceless, and we are not simply a body-mind. Therefore the emphasis is not on attainment, or some spiritual evolution which keeps the ego thriving, but seeing what we are not. When the mind is free of its encumbrances we are open to what is beyond the mind. He would often use Heidegger's phrase 'waiting without waiting'. We are in a place of availability open to light, to grace. But there is not the slightest emphasis on waiting for something or a somebody waiting.

It might be asked: *How does coming to know myself, to know truth, change the world?* But it is only when we know ourselves that there is real intelligence, and hence the clarity to act in the world. Otherwise, we're part of the problem. Free of the 'me', the person, there is love, and action will be for the good of the whole. There is no separation. You are the world.

THE ART OF LISTENING

At the heart of this approach, whether it concerns self knowledge or coming to know the body, is how we observe: the art of listening. Listening here is not confined to hearing with the ears but refers to our total receptivity.

In unconditioned listening, choiceless listening, we are completely open. It is an openness free of purpose or intent. It is an innocent welcoming of all that appears. It is like a scientist without presuppositions, just open to the facts.

However, we rarely listen in this impersonal way. It is the nature of the ego to grasp and look for security in what is observed. Instead of just looking we interpret, analyse, judge, compare or lose ourselves in the feeling or thought. When we are looking for something from the perception, there is end-gaining and we are caught in the becoming process.

Instead of seeing what is, we only see what we want to see, our own projections. The ego is always choosing what brings it pleasure and discarding what brings it pain.

We are too dominated by the conceptual mind (abstraction) and live too little in direct seeing. Instead of staying with the perception we jump too quickly to the concept; instead of really seeing the flower, letting its richness unfold and feeling the sense of wonder, we are too quick to name it and categorise it. Thus the senses become atrophied, we cut ourselves off from the totality and we live in our own isolated conceptual world. We should take note of this tendency as it happens: just seeing it will help to break the pattern. This is not some mental taking note, but a seeing of the situation and feeling how it acts on us, how it feels to be the seer. In taking note we are free from the pattern.

When we maintain this open quality of attention, the perceived increasingly recedes and we are more aware of listening itself. We discover that this unconditioned listening is our real nature.

Jean would often remind us to bring the perceived back to the perceiving; to bring the seen to the seeing, the heard to the hearing, the felt to the feeling, to bring back each object to its homeground. Objects are not outside of us, they have their potential in us, and so when the energy is no longer directed, when the emphasis is no longer on the seen, it naturally and without volition, dissolves back in the seeing. We find ourselves in the seeing; consciousness and perceiving are one, there is nothing outside of us. Listening cannot be localised—it is beyond space and time.

> *In this observing is the total absence of yourself.*
> *It is your real presence.*
>
> Jean Klein, *Living Truth*

LISTENING TO THE BODY

Listening begins with the immediate environment, the body. When we come to a freedom in the body we're more open to listening to our wider environment. Ultimately listening refers to itself, and not to any object of listening; we *are* the listening.

So first we face the fact of the body. We know the body mostly through sensation, the tactile feeling. We let the sensation awaken and come to us.

We don't truly know the real body; rather, what we experience when we wake up in the morning is largely memory. It is a pattern crystallised over time, more or less a set of defence mechanisms for the I-image. This set of patterns that pervades every layer of the body unknowingly imprisons us in our past. It is frozen energy that gives us the feeling of contraction, weight, opacity and fixation. We are, more particularly, localised in the forebrain, the thought factory. In the real body, the global body, the I-image loses its hold.

We don't listen to the body from the head, but from our wholeness. It is impossible to experience the whole body from the head since our head is part of the whole. This listening needs no effort; choiceless listening is the natural function of awareness. Any anticipation or intention only interferes. In anticipation there is end-gaining, becoming; we're back in the mind, no longer in the moment.

To become acquainted with the body, wait, and let the sensation awaken and speak to you. From the gross feeling of contraction and density, to the subtle feeling of vibration and space, we pass through various layers. As we let the layers of sensation unfold, the body will go through various stages of elimination. In this process we will discover that our primal body is vibration—subtle energy without centre or border.

Jean compared the body to a musical instrument; by listening we come to tune it, we come to harmonisation.

In listening to the body in this way, a choiceless welcoming, we are no longer an accomplice to the patterns and contractions. We have, as it were, stood back and let the body *be* the body. We are no longer fuelling the reactions. There is a feeling of space between awareness and what we're aware of, a feeling of detachment—but without trying to be detached.

There is listening before we listen to the body, there is listening after. The body unfolds in listening and since we don't emphasise what we listen to, once it has told its story it naturally dissolves back into awareness. The presence of the body in awareness is discontinuous, but awareness, the background, is continuous.

The body is thus a pointer to awareness. The purpose of all objects is to remind us of our real nature: awareness, consciousness. The world is thus not a problem, but a continual reminder of who we are. We can also say that all so-called objects are consciousness celebrating itself.

Listening to the body gives freedom to the body, and familiarises us with the art of listening.

> *To an ignorant man the objective world is an obstacle to spiritual progress, because objects always draw him away from his centre, which has not yet been shown to him. But to one who has heard the truth from his Guru, the same world serves as a help to his spiritual progress, since each of its objects points to his real nature.*
>
> Shri Atmananda (Krishna Menon),
> *Notes on Spiritual Discourses*

In pure listening there is not an object listened to—which would be a concept—but simply feeling, seeing, hearing, smelling and tasting. Neither is there a listener, which would be another concept. Consciousness and its object are one; it is only after the experience that we divide the seer from the seen. We say, 'I saw the tree', 'I acted in the situation', but at the moment of seeing there is only seeing, at the moment of action there is only acting. The seer, the seeing and the seen are one. Ultimately we come to realise that the body and all manifestation are nothing but awareness.

The centre of this approach is based on listening and not on the attainment of some goal in some future time. Our real nature is non-objective, beyond space and time, we are already free, but we don't know ourselves in this freedom. When there is no understanding of this we are inevitably trapped in ideas of progress and seeking experiences. When we don't question the initial premise, 'I am a personal entity', all subsequent practices only reinforce our false sense of self. Over time, we may eliminate various layers and focus on more and more subtle experiences, but even the experience of nothingness is still an experience and remains on the objective level. By 'object' I mean something that is either perceived or conceived, be it a table, the body, thought, memory. But what we are in our essential nature can never be an object, can never be known in terms of the senses or mind. All that can be obtained is an object; when we truly realise the full implication of this fact there is a stop, a giving up of all striving and a re-orchestration of our energy.

It may appear in this approach that we are emphasising the body. This is only apparently so, as the real emphasis is on listening itself and not what we are listening to.

Some people found Jean's teaching on the verbal level difficult to fully comprehend, but through the body work they came to a feeling of non-localisation and to a glimpse of their real nature: complete openness, free of the dichotomy of inside and outside.

Until there is real understanding, our body, senses and mind, including our breathing, reflect the egoistic state, which manifests as contraction, defence, grasping and fear. So in the following pages we will be focusing on different practices to free us from what we are not. Because we are so identified with a particular body-mind that we call 'myself,' we are asked to let it be an object in awareness. We are only the witness to the unfolding perception. This brings a feeling of space, a detachment from what we have habitually taken ourselves to be. This division between subject, which is the listener, and object, what is listened to, is an important pedagogical device until we realise that the body and the whole of the manifest world are expressions of consciousness, and as such nothing other than consciousness. There are never actually two.

Of course, for normal functioning the body needs a certain tension, otherwise we'd collapse. This is physiological tension that is part of normal muscle functioning; the problem arises when the tension is psychological and based on fear, resistance and habit.

The layers of tension in the body are often chronic and deep-seated; they may have built up over many years. They are not going to dissolve overnight; this approach needs time and dedication. However, the cells of the body have an organic memory and once we discover our original body the new feeling invites us. Ultimately we need to understand the nature of this resistance, how the imaginary 'I' creates it.

We can learn to relax the body-mind but the ultimate relaxation can only be when we know our real nature.

THE PROCESS OF LETTING GO

Although there may be part of us that really wants to let go, there may be another part that has a deep fear of releasing the tensions and patterns that have colonised our body-mind over many years. So we need not be too surprised that when we begin to release certain surface tensions a feeling of disorientation or even sensations of panic arise. So, what is happening? The chronic tensions and resistances in our body have been built up to defend who we think we are. When we begin to release them there arises also a fear of losing this identity or a feeling of being defenceless. It is a fear of the unknown, for who would I be without weight and density, this armour and the walls I have built up around me? The more we understand that this fear is based on an illusion, that the self-image, the ego, has no more reality than a phantom, the more we will effortlessly give up what we are not. There is nobody giving up, it happens by itself.

In this process of letting go feelings and emotions of joy and release may arise, but in the beginning, it may also be otherwise. Buried in the structure of the body and in our breathing habits can be traumas dating back to childhood, perhaps from a dominating father or frightening authority figure. When we begin to release this frozen energy, the emotions that were originally associated with this contraction may manifest themselves. There may arise anger, there may arise tears.

It is important to allow that which needs to surface, to surface and not to suppress feelings, but to give space for the body to free itself. There is no need to analyse and delve into what might be the origin of these feelings, but just allow the sensation to unfold and have its say. Otherwise we return to our conceptual world and interfere with this cleansing process. Can I be the uninvolved witness of this releasing process? The body knows its own health and, when allowed, will free itself from all residues. There are no rules as to how long this process takes; it depends on the baggage we are carrying and our commitment to self-exploring.

When the neuromuscular contractions begin to free themselves there may arise a series of jerks or something that feels like electrical impulses in the body. This is nothing uncommon or anything to worry about. This process may also become more elaborate and take on a variety of forms, such as the head shaking spontaneously from side to side or the body swaying or going into spontaneous movements. This happens only when we allow it and we can stop the process at any time. It is a process where the tensions in the body are unwinding and releasing restrictions.

Over time, the release of gross tensions allows the more subtle energies to flow in the body. Although there is no outward movement, these energies can be surprisingly strong. It is important to allow them, for this is a deep cleansing of the whole psychosomatic structure. These energies may be experienced more intensely at certain energy centres (chakras) or as upward-flowing energy from the base of the spine or as pressure in the head. This may come in waves, or build up as behind a dam, before flowing through. These strong energy flows can also be experienced throughout the body not just along the central energy channels. They may sometimes be accompanied by seeing light.

Generally these releases are not overwhelming or unpleasant; the body in its wisdom will release what we are comfortable with. Don't indulge in what may be very pleasant sensations; they are objects like any other. Don't be lost in them, otherwise they become a distraction—sweets for the ego. You are the witness. They are not our concern here; they are merely a by-product as we become more harmonious in our being.

There may be techniques to open the chakras using the will, but these are completely artificial. It is with understanding that the natural opening of the centres occurs.

> *Beware of promises, pleasures and powers achieved or anticipated.*
>
> *All these seduce you from the truth.*
>
> Shri Atmananda (Krishna Menon),
> *Notes on Spiritual Discourses*

GIVING WEIGHT TO THE GROUND:
SHAVASANA

Before we feel our lightness and spaciousness we should first experience the heaviness of the body and give up this weight to the ground. It's not just weight we are giving up, it's our defences, the psychological 'me'. When there are deep-seated tensions in the body it may take some time and practice to allow a letting go of the weight of the different parts of the body to the ground. These tensions can be so ingrained that we may hardly be aware of them.

> Lying on the floor:
>
> Feel where the body touches the ground; feel the different points of contact, heels, calves, thighs and buttocks, where the weight is given.
>
> Feel each area in turn. Take your time.
>
> Do you really release the weight?

Feel the whole contact your feet and legs make.

Feel their heaviness, let them fall away from you.

Now feel the contact of your hands, forearms, upper arms and shoulders.

Can you let them go as if they don't belong to you?

Feel the contact of the hips; it may take time to feel the release.

Allow your back to spread over the ground.

Feel the contact of your head, can you let the ground carry it, or are you holding on to it?

Now feel all the points of contact fusing into one feeling of contact.

Feel the body entering the ground.

Feel the ground entering the body.

Feel them as one.

When we do release, the actual area of contact increases, as the tense muscles give up their hold.

*

Some alternatives to help release of the body, lying on the floor:

Tensing—releasing

Tense and release each part of the body in turn. You can inhale with the contraction and exhale with the release.

Begin with your hands, make fists with your hands and release.

Stretch your fingers open and release.

Tense up your shoulders towards your ears and let go.

Now tense your hands, arms and shoulders together and let go.

Continue with your toes, feet, legs, buttocks and then all these simultaneously.

Tense up the abdominal area and release.

Now, in turn, the mouth, eyes, whole face, and then whole body.

You can tense and release each part three times. What is important is to feel the effect after the exercise.

*

Lifting—Dropping

Lift the right arm off the ground about 30 cm (twelve inches) with the inhalation and let it fall, letting go completely with the exhalation.

Now with the left.

Keeping the knee a little bent, lift the right leg with the inhalation. This lift should be only a few centimeters so as not to hurt your heel. Let the leg fall with the exhalation.

Repeat with the left.

You can do this several times with each limb.

*

Lifting—Placing

With each inhale lift each limb in turn a little off the ground, hold it a moment and then place it slowly on the ground with the exhale.

Experience its weight.

Do the same with the head.

With each exhalation you can also let your head roll

to one side, as if falling. Return to the centre slowly with the inhale and proceed to the other side with the next exhale.

*

Letting go with each exhalation

We can use the exhalation to help us release tension in the body.

> Be aware of your breath and with each exhale feel the letting go of your hands.

> With each exhalation feel a letting go of your arms.

> Proceed through your body, each area in turn, allowing release with each out-breath.

> *Generally our contact with the ground is passive. But when we see that there is contact and a counter-contact, that is, body and ground are interwoven—the body goes in the ground and the ground goes in the body—when this happens there is no longer resistance or opposition. Then there is harmonisation of energy. Our body is no longer felt as separate from global energy, but is integrated in the living ground and the ground is integrated in our body.*
>
> Jean Klein, *The Book of Listening*

Once we release the weight, along with the tensions and

resistances, we are more available to the subtle energies of the body. A relaxed body is a beginning, but this relaxed body, the corpse pose, is an inert body. We need to explore more deeply to come to the living body, the energetic body with its dynamism.

LETTING THE SENSATION UNFOLD

Once we have learnt to let go and come to the relaxed body we can begin the exercise in the following pages.

As before, we first give up the weight of the body to the ground. We then let the feeling of the different parts of the body come alive—we let them be sensation. However, the real feeling of the body—one of transparency and spaciousness—is often paralysed, and it may be this fixation that we first encounter when listening to the body. But once we release the holding, the body as sensation begins to awaken.

It cannot be stated too strongly that once we slip from feeling the sensation to having a concept of the body, we are in memory, which is an abstraction. We are not with what is—the living present. When this happens we simply fix the body and nothing can change or unfold; the layers of the body stay frozen in time.

Take the example of fear: instead of staying with the feeling and allowing it—whether it is the tension in the abdomen, shoulders or jaw, or a restriction in the breathing—we resist it and create another layer of reaction, so that we have a double reaction. We now call this fixed tension 'fear', but we are no longer with the fear but the concept of fear. If we could make friends with the initial feeling and allow its expression in the body, then, we give the fixed energy the possibility to unfold and free itself. It should be clear that we cannot feel and think at the same time, although we may have the impression that we do so. So in this acceptance of the sensation we are no longer an accomplice to its creation—it can unfold and reintegrate in the whole. At this point we don't emphasise what is accepted or even the integrated body feeling, but the accepting itself—we feel ourselves in welcoming and in this there is freedom. We are one with the welcoming.

Often in yoga classes there is a certain lip service paid to the importance of sensing the body, feeling each part in turn and going quickly to the next. When we proceed in this way we are largely caught in memory, an idea of the body, for it takes time, especially in the beginning, for the different layers of sensation to unfold and blossom. Rushing through the body takes us nowhere. So in the following exercise take all the time you need.

> Lying on the floor:

> Beginning with the left hand, experience each finger in turn.

> Feel the space between the fingers.

> Feel the palm of the hand, the surface feeling, the tactile sensation.

Feel the back of the hand.

Now the whole hand; you may feel a tingling, a warmth.

Don't fix the sensation. There are many layers so let it continue to unfold moment to moment. Give it time.

Feel the whole volume, the space it occupies. Feel it merging with the space around. Perhaps you experience it as more spacious than in your visual memory.

At this point it would be interesting to compare the feeling of the left hand with the right. You may be surprised by the difference.

Now proceed in the same way with the right hand.

Then feel both.

We begin with the hands because the energy feeling is particularly strong in the hands. The energy body permeates the physical body and extends into the space around. When it comes alive it eats up the feeling of solidity of the body so here we may feel as if the hands disappear.

From your left hand go upwards through your wrist, forearm, upper arm, shoulder and experience each area in turn.

Now feel the whole arm. Feel it without thinking it.

You can compare the arms.

Proceed with the right arm. (You could also feel both hands and arms simultaneously.)

Then feel both arms.

Feel the left foot, the sole of the foot, the upper part, the surface sensation and then the complete feeling.

Let it unfold—give it space.

Compare it with the right.

Then proceed with the right in the same way.

Now with both legs: starting from your feet, go upwards—ankles, lower legs, knees, upper legs, hips and buttocks.

Come to the complete feeling of your legs.

Experience the lumbar back, feel the radiation, the warmth, spreading over the floor.

Feel the dorsal back and the radiation spreading over the floor.

Feel the abdomen and chest; do they move freely with the flow of the breath?

Listen to the back of your neck; you can visualise a warm hand resting here. Can you feel a softness, a warmth? Let the sensation of your face awaken; feel the mask that covers over the real face, experience all the tension you hold here; welcome it and let it unfold.

Feel it melting like wax in the sun.

Then just feel it as a mass of warmth.

Feel the whole back of your body.

Feel the whole front.

Feel your body as one.

Can you experience your body as homogeneous: the same quality pervading the whole body? This may not come for some time.

Does it have any definite borders?

There may be certain parts of our body that we don't feel, that are unconscious; we will need to return to these parts often until they begin to speak to us. We can use visualisation or simply touch these areas with our hands to bring more life. When we visualise part of the body, it involves a certain abstraction which involves memory. But to *feel* is a direct perception with no thinking involved. However, if we first visualise the body, or parts of it, it may help us to subsequently feel the body as sensation, as an energy field.

When the sensation has completely unfolded, given up all its secrets, the sensation is allowed to dissolve in awareness. We no longer emphasise the object, that which we are aware of, but awareness itself. By 'emphasise awareness', I mean, *be* the awareness knowingly. In fact you can never not be this.

THE OPENING OF THE SENSES

We perceive the world through the five senses and, through what we could call the sixth sense—the mind—we conceive it. There is no problem in this, except when we are identified with a particular body-mind. In this identification, thought and the function of the senses are commandeered to support and defend this territory. The ego centre, by its very nature, is fragile, and unreal; thus it can never be completely relaxed. For example, the eyes will tend to grasp objects instead of welcoming what appears. The eyes, and hence the brain, expend large amounts of energy unnecessarily. Instead of simply seeing, touching, smelling, tasting and hearing we quickly conceptualise the world: when we see a sunset, instead of living with the experience, we immediately call it 'beautiful' and are therefore no longer with the beauty. In the same way, we conceptualise ourselves and those around us. Our senses become programmed and lazy, dominated by memory, and thus we become almost incapable of experiencing life in its freshness, moment to moment. We become alienated from the world around us and from ourselves, living in a conceptual universe of our own making. Freeing the senses of their contraction begins a rehabilitation of our sensory world and allows us to experience life afresh.

*

The mouth

Often the jaw and cheeks, with the associated muscles of mastication, are in constant tension. What is this saying about ourselves? Is this aggression, defence or living in constant anticipation or a habit we've become blind to? We will need to shine the light of awareness often to free ourselves of the encumbrances we carry.

When our mouth is relaxed our experience of tasting food has a different quality; also the tensions in our inner ears are released.

To discover a relaxed mouth, relaxed senses, and ultimately a transparent body has a deeply liberating effect.

> Be aware of your face, let it be sensation.
>
> Where are you holding tension?
>
> It's there because you are maintaining it; in just being aware of it and letting it unfold you give it the opportunity to dissolve.
>
> How does your jaw feel?

Let your lower jaw fall a little away from the upper jaw.

Feel the sensation of your lips, your teeth and gums.

Feel the whole inner walls of your mouth.

Feel your tongue: where exactly is it in your mouth?

Feel your tongue like a large wet sponge resting on the floor of your mouth, inside your lower teeth.

Relax the root of your tongue; see how this affects your throat.

Visualise a peach filling your mouth, and feel the effect.

Feel the volume of your mouth and allow its spaciousness.

How does the relaxation of your mouth affect you?

Imagine some salt on your tongue, let the taste come, now the taste of the mouth itself.

Imagine some honey, let the taste come, experience it. Now just the taste of the mouth itself.

The mouth has its own taste.

*

The ears

The ears—like the eyes—tend to grasp, looking for the familiar, for security. We seldom listen innocently but when we do—for example, when listening to music—and receive it with our totality, with our whole body, this can have a profound effect. It brings us to spaciousness and reminds us of our real nature.

> Let the sensation of your left ear awaken, go inside, be aware of the tension you hold.
>
> Feel the architecture, the space of your ear.
>
> Feel the sensation, the vibration; wait for it to come to you.
>
> Feel the space like a large cave.
>
> Likewise with your right ear.
>
> Now both ears.
>
> Feel the spaces merging, filling your head.
>
> Let your whole body become your ears.
>
> Hear the sounds around you with your whole body.
>
> Let the sound come to you without naming or choosing.

Let your hearing be pure hearing, where nothing is heard and nobody is hearing.

There is just hearing, where you are the hearing.

*

The Inner Sound:

Listen to the inner sound, let it come without effort.

The body has its own vibration; we can hear it, but only when we become very quiet.

*

Sound Inside or Outside?

Hear the sound around you.

Is the sound that you hear inside you or outside you?

Is there really an inside and an outside?

Is there really any division?

When the sense organs are freed from past conditioning they cease grasping, de-contract and are receptive to the newness of every moment. When hearing something take note that you fix the sound. Let it go. There must be no concentration. In this non-directed hearing, this multidimensional hearing, many sounds will be heard in succession. Without your choosing or showing any particular preference for any particular noise, you may observe that they are eliminated until only one sound remains. If you do not focus on this sound it also dies away and you find yourself in pure listening. In the same way, when all the taste is eliminated from your mouth, you arrive at the taste of the mouth itself. But to return to hearing, in the end, it reabsorbs itself completely into pure awareness.

Jean Klein, *I Am*

*

The skin

The skin is the largest and heaviest organ of the body. It's apparently where 'I' end and the world outside begins. It's symbolic of the frontier of what is me and what is not me. By exploring, as in all of these exercises, we may alleviate our sense of division.

> Lying on the floor (if you prefer to sit you can adapt the following instructions), allow a letting-go throughout your body.
>
> Feel the skin, the surface of your body.
>
> Feel where you touch your clothes, the ground, the air around you.

Now let us go slowly: feel the tips of your fingers, feel the skin covering your fingers.

Feel the palms of your hands, the back of your hands, the whole covering of your hands; the tactile sensation.

It may feel warm or cool, a sense of tingling, energy or vibration or something more vague. Just stay with whatever presents itself without naming or judging.

Staying with this surface feeling of the body, feel the forearms, upper arms and round your shoulders.

During this exercise it may help you at times to visualise some warm liquid moving over your body to bring more aliveness to specific areas, or warm hands touching you.

Feel the whole covering of your arms.

Feel the skin covering your toes, the soles of your feet, the upper part, and now the entire surface of your feet.

Proceed, feeling the skin covering the following areas:

Your lower legs, upper legs and hips.

This whole area.

The abdominal area, front, sides and back.

The chest, front, sides and back.

Now your neck.

Experience the surface of your face, the cheeks, lips, temples, forehead, scalp, eyebrows and now the whole face. Feel your face like a thin veil.

Now feel the whole surface of your body, this tactile feeling.

From the surface, go deeper to experience a more complete feeling of the body.

Now, again from the surface, feel the warmth and radiation of your body filling the space around you.

Stay with this feeling of expansion.

Does your body really have any definite border?

How does the exercise affect you?

Feel your oneness with the space around you.

*

The Nostrils

Feel the space of the left nostril.

Feel the tension you hold here.

Feel the touch of the air.

And now similarly with the right nostril.

Feel the difference in temperature of the inhalation and exhalation.

Follow the rhythm of the breath.

Be aware of any tendency to grasp or push the breath.

Let the breath come and go without interference.

Feel the energy, the *prana*, that is within the air, like the current within an electric cable.

Let yourself be breathed.

*

The Eyes

Either lying or sitting:

Allow the feeling of your eyes to awaken.

Feel their weight.

Feel the tension you hold in your eyes, stay with it, let it unfold, and let it melt away.

Feel the space of the left eye socket.

Feel its concavity.

Now experience the left eye itself.

Let the eye fill the socket.

Proceed with the right eye in the same way.

Now feel both eyes.

Feel them like globes filling the front of your face.

Go very slowly. This all takes time or it will be of no benefit.

Whilst lying on your back, feel the weight of your eyes falling back inside your head.

Whilst sitting, feel as if your eyes are expanded several centimetres in front of you.

Our bodies, the muscles and the nervous system, react differently according to our environment; for example, when we are looking out into the open sea compared to looking at a building.

With your eyes closed visualise a large rock several metres in front of you.

How does this affect you?

*

Visualise an expansive landscape spreading out in front of you.

With your whole being, open yourself to it, go into it, touch it with the tactile sensation.

Note how it affects you.

We waste a great deal of energy through tension in the eyes, which directly affects the brain. Note how the relaxation of the eyes affects the brain, and the whole psychosomatic structure.

When we are without motive and are not grasping with the eyes or other sense organs, they become relaxed and we let the world come to us. When we are totally open, available and not naming, we experience seeing, hearing, touching, smelling, tasting with our whole body. Sensing is no longer restricted to the particular sense organ. In pure perception we are open to the sense of wonder. More profoundly, when the senses are no longer conditioned by a perceiver, objects are no longer objects; they are extensions of ourselves, expressions of silence.

Can you respond with all your senses; when you respond with only one particular sense, in that response there's division, breaking up. Can you look at the sea with all your senses, the tasting, the smelling, the touching, the feel. When you do that there is no centre from where you're holistically responding. Our life is so short, and in this brief period we must learn only to observe. To observe without the flow of thought, observe without time, observe without knowledge of the past, without the observer, who is the essence of the past. Look attentively, look at the clouds, look at the birds, it's all part of life. When we look attentively, diligently, there's nothing to learn, there is only the immense space, the silence, the void, which is the energy which all consumes.

J. Krishnamurti

*

Eye exercises

Sitting in a comfortable position, follow the suggestions in the previous pages and come to the relaxed feeling of your eyes.

These exercises are done without moving the head.

Open your eyes and, without straining, look slowly to the left and slowly to the right, about five times in each direction.

Between each exercise close your eyes and let them relax completely.

Open your eyes, look upwards and downwards and then close your eyes.

Open your eyes and look up diagonally right, down diagonally left and close.

And now the other diagonal, up left, down right, and close.

Open your eyes and go round in large circles clockwise and then anti-clockwise and close. How smoothly do your eyes rotate?

Blink your eyes, opening and closing. And now do it a little faster.

Close your eyes tightly, open them wide, let all the light in. Do it several times.

Close your eyes gently; it's just the weight of your eyelids closing.

And now palm your eyes, covering them with the palms of your hands to exclude all light. There should be no pressure on the eyes from the hands. Let your eyes rest in the darkness.

How do you experience your eyes after the exercise?

> When you open your eyes don't look at things, rather let things come to you, seeing without grasping.

*

Healing with colour

Each colour has its own properties and has its own impact on us. As with sound, colour affects us not just physically but also on the emotional level. This is why we can use colour, with the help of visualisation, for healing.

We will visualise certain colours and feel how they affect us.

> First close your eyes and come to the relaxed feeling of your eyes.
>
> Visualise the colour green, bring this colour to your eyes, let them bathe in it.
>
> Cover your whole body with green.
>
> How does this colour affect you?
>
> Let green fade away slowly.
>
> Now visualise yellow, and proceed as above.
>
> You can continue with blue and perhaps finish with white or choose colours which you feel your body needs.

To help you visualise you can imagine a green meadow or a blue sky, or imagine yourself inside a room painted white.

Experiment with different colours and feel their psychosomatic impact.

*

The brain

The habitual dominance of the I-image in our psychology means the brain feels contracted, only functioning within repeated patterns. Sensing the brain frees these patterns and has a deep effect on the whole body-mind.

Before exploring the sensation of the brain it is helpful to first come to the relaxed feeling of the eyes. You can experience your brain as you can any other part of your body.

> Let your eyes close. Can you feel the weight of your brain?
>
> Let the sensation of the left hemisphere of your brain awaken, feel its vibration.
>
> Feel it expand to fill the whole left side of your head, feel it like a large mushroom.
>
> Do the same with the right hemisphere.

Feel both sides, feel them as one.

Feel the fluid that surrounds your brain, feel it floating in the liquid.

Feel how sensing the brain frees us from thinking, since thinking is a localisation in the forehead. Sensing the brain frees us from ourselves.

WHAT WE TAKE IN

Jean was sometimes asked about diet. He did not prescribe a particular diet but advised us to be sensitive to the effect of all we take in. He stressed the importance of natural unprocessed food, particularly raw, 'living' food and whole grains. He also spoke about how we should combine different foods.

> *Modern man is a creature whose digestive tract and mind are practically always overcrowded. (There is a strong link between these two types of overcrowding.) The first thing is to relieve the mind and abstain from treating it like a garbage can into which are poured all the residues of radio, television, the daily press and detective novels.*
>
> *The second is not to treat one's stomach as a receptacle which is undiscerningly crammed with all the products of the modern food industry.*
>
> Jean Klein, *Be Who You Are*

The path of self-knowing asks for the utmost sensitivity to ourselves; stimulants, and nutrition that makes us heavy and dull, are hardly appropriate. Right eating, on the contrary, brings a sense of lightness and alertness.

Everything we take in can either enhance or disturb our psychosomatic structure; that is why art and beauty are profoundly important.

Our essential nature is beauty. Art, in the pure sense, be it music, painting, poetry, sculpture or architecture, comes from beauty. When we are in the presence of art and let it take us, we live in beauty and this reminds us of our own beauty. All objects are reminders of ourselves, but objects of art bring us actively to ourselves. This beauty is beyond all representation, beyond time and space.

DISCOVERING OUR VERTICALITY:

RIGHT SITTING

Correct sitting is the foundation of any meditative practice or *pranayama*.

You can sit on the ground, with perhaps a cushion or meditation stool, or in a chair that allows you to sit straight. What is important is that you are comfortable and you're able to keep your spine straight. It may take some time before you are able to sit like this without strain or fatigue; however, it is the most natural way to sit.

> Feel where the weight of your body meets the ground.
>
> Feel where your sit bones rest; be sure you don't sway back onto your coccyx, rather let it float.
>
> Feel where your feet and legs rest and the contact they make with the ground.

Feel the contact of your hands where they are at rest.

Allow the weight of your arms and shoulders to drop into the contact of your hands.

Be aware of the tension you hold in your face, allow it to dissolve.

Let your whole body be alive for you; feel the different parts and come to the feeling of openness.

Feel your verticality.

Don't try to make yourself straight, only let the feeling bring you to verticality.

If you make yourself straight by imposing it through will and muscular tension, you will block the inner sensitivity. Thus the real verticality will be replaced by an artificial one, which will eventually sag through fatigue.

From the base of your spine, travel upwards with your awareness through the dorsal, thoracic and cervical sections.

Feel each vertebra floating in its own space.

Feel the independence of the thoracic region, the rib cage floating above the abdominal area, and not collapsing into it.

Feel your neck like a swan's.

Feel your head as a continuation of your spine.

Visualise your head like a large balloon, floating in space.

There is a tendency to tighten the back of the neck, pushing the chin forward and the top of the head backwards.

To counteract this, feel the back of your neck, now visualise placing the back of your neck against a flat piece of wood.

Or imagine it like a drawer being drawn backwards. You will feel the back of your neck lengthening and the chin coming slightly inside.

Now feel the back of your neck covering the wall behind you.

We generally keep a lot of tension in our shoulders. Sometimes they are permanently raised without us realising it.

Are your shoulders really down?

Consciously lift your shoulders and allow them to sink slowly all the way down; do it several times.

You can visualise warm hands resting on your shoulders,

feel their weight, the warmth.

See how it affects your shoulders.

Have the feeling of your collarbones flying outwards to the sides, or as wings.

Let your shoulder blades fall together in your back, and now feel them coming forward, deeper into your back.

It is important to take your time and feel the effect of each instruction or visualisation, otherwise it remains dead.

*

The following further instructions and visualisations can be used on occasion.

Visualise your spine as an elevator going up and your shoulders as elevators going down.

Feel this double direction.

*

You can also work from above: visualise yourself as a puppet, with a string attached to the crown of your head. Feel it pulling you upwards, your whole spine following, feel your elasticity.

*

In your verticality there is the correct balance of tension operating in your spine. There is space for your lungs to breathe, for each organ to function and for energy to flow. It brings alertness and facilitates our ultimate openness.

Of course, the spine is by no means straight; it is a series of curves. Without its curvature we could not function. The problem is when we let it collapse through bad posture, perhaps sitting at a desk all day, and we create exaggerated curvature, kyphosis of the thoracic spine or lordosis of the lumbar.

Maybe there is a feeling that your spine wants to collapse; allow it to collapse, as if you're sinking into a comfortable armchair. Go with the sinking, staying with the feeling, sinking and then rising. It is because you have not deeply felt your body and so it is not truly alive, that sitting straight seems an effort. You must discover an effortless verticality.

> Visualise a straight line through the axis of your body.
> Now let your body accommodate itself to the line.

*

> Visualise a straight line in front of you.
> Now feel it in your centre.

*

Visualise your spine like a water fountain from the base to the top of your head.

Now feel this water going down over your shoulders, and over your arms, taking them lower.

*

Visualise breathing in from the base of your spine towards the crown of your head, feeling each in-breath make you straight.

Feel each out-breath from the crown of your head, towards the ceiling—making you still straighter.

THE BREATH—LETTING IT FLOW

In taking ourselves to be a separate entity, fear and insecurity arise. When we separate ourselves from life there is defence, often without us really being aware of it. These patterns inevitably manifest themselves in our breath. The breath is a barometer of our psychosomatic state. The body breathes perfectly well without our interference. But instead of letting the breath come to us there is a tendency to grasp the inhalation and a refusal to let go of the exhalation. Before the exhalation has completed itself we are already inhaling. So instead of our breathing being spontaneous, physiological, it becomes a psychological arena.

Our breathing in these exercises should be through the nostrils; they are specially constructed to filter, warm and humidify the air before it enters the lungs.

Sitting or lying:

Without wishing to change anything be aware of the flow of your breath.

Even in simply observing your breath there may be a tendency to interfere with the flow, but this will soon disappear.

Let each inhalation come to you, let each exhalation dissolve.

Each in-breath is a gift.

Each out-breath is an offering.

No one is offering, there is just offering.

Be clear with yourself whether your breathing is really spontaneous or there is some manipulation happening.

There may be a tendency to take the in-breath and to push the out-breath.

Just take note of this tendency.

*

The space between each breath

Sitting or lying:

Be aware of the space, the void at the end of the out-breath.

Do you allow this resting space or is there a jump to

breathe in?

Allow this space, this tranquil moment in your breathing.

Attune yourself to this moment, be one with it.

Let yourself dissolve with this out-breath.

When there is a complete letting go of the out-breath, then the in-breath has a different quality.

From the point of view of the mind this space is empty and lasts a moment, but from the perspective of reality it is full and timeless.

Don't make an object of this space, you are one with it, you are in identity with it.

It is the stillness from where the breath comes and into which it dissolves back.

Silence is the constant background; the breath is superimposed on this silence. The breath is an expression of silence and also ultimately one with it. The expressions of consciousness are nothing other than consciousness, there are not two.

*

Many of the spiritual practices in this book have echoes of the *Vijnana Bhairava* (Divine Consciousness), a book from the non-dualistic Shaivite tradition of Kashmir, perhaps dating from the 7th century CE. This was a favourite text of Jean Klein and several verses are quoted in the appendix to this book.

*

Exploring our capacity to breathe: sensing it in different parts

Restricted patterns of breathing develop when we close down part of our capacity to breath. This may be the result of trauma, chronic fear or bad posture. It means, for example, that tightness in the abdominal region interferes with the free movement of the diaphragm and hence restricts breathing in the abdominal area. Strictly speaking, there is no such thing as abdominal breathing since the lungs purely occupy the thoracic region, but we feel the movement of the diaphragm and the abdominal organs responding to the breath.

The lungs are one space, expanding and contracting, but to realise their capacity it is helpful to explore each area in turn before feeling the space as one.

We will now explore breathing in the different parts of the lungs and encourage its expansion. We are just exploring the breath, without interfering or wishing to control it.

Sitting or lying:

Feel the movement of the breath in the abdominal region. First feel it in the front, feel the rise and fall of your belly with each inhalation and each exhalation.

Is this area nourished by breath? Is the rhythm smooth?

Do you feel space after the in-breath?

Do you feel space after the out-breath?

You can also place your hands on the different areas we explore to make it clearer for you.

Still focusing in the abdominal area, experience the breath in the sides and then the back.

Feel the effect of the breath in this whole circle, like a tyre round the abdominal area.

Now moving up to the thoracic area, feel the breath in the front, feel the elasticity of the rib cage, the upward and outward movements.

Feel the breath in the sides, the back and in the circle.

Moving higher, feel the breath in the clavicular region, the upper most part of the lungs.

Feel it in the front; do you allow the breath in this part?

Feel it in the sides, the back and in the circle.

Now feel the whole rhythm of the breath, feel the expansion with the in-breath—first in the abdominal area, then through the thoracic and into the clavicular.

And with the out-breath feel the emptying from the clavicular through the thoracic to the abdominal.

Some people have what is known as paradoxical breathing, when the abdomen sinks with the inhale and expands with the exhale. There may be certain medical conditions that cause this, but it can also be the result of chronic tensions in the abdominal area.

*

Taking charge of the breath: expanding the breath

Sitting or lying:

Breathe consciously into the abdominal area for several long, deep breaths.

Now focus just in the thoracic area, again with deep breathing, and then in the clavicular area.

Using the whole capacity of the lungs, inhale from the base to the top, and exhale from the top through to the base.

Maintain the same density in the breath.

Respect the space between each breath.

Do you really go to the end with the exhalation?

Do you really fill the whole lungs with the inhalation?

Be sure there is no strain; find an effortlessness in your breathing.

Now don't control the breathing at all—simply observe the quality.

When you become very still the breath also becomes very still.

To begin with you can do this exercise for a few minutes and then, when you are more comfortable with it, you can extend the time.

*

Whole body as breath

Sitting or lying:

Be aware of your whole body: your body as sensation, the global feeling.

Feel the breath in the different parts.

Feel the breath in your whole body, feel the whole body as breath, your body as an inhalation and an exhalation.

You're not controlling, just observing.

*

The expansion of the breath in space

Sitting:

With the eyes closed, visualise the space in front of you.

Now visualise the breath in this space.

Visualise the space behind you.

Then visualise breathing in this space behind you.

Do the same with the space to the left and right.

Spend a minute or two, or preferably longer, in each space.

Now experience the breath in this total expansion.

Repeat the exercise but this time with deep breathing in each space and in your global feeling.

And now, no longer just visualising, feel your breathing completely non-localised.

Now leave your breath to its own rhythm and take note of how you feel.

Real breathing is in space, non-localised.

No longer focusing on your breath, let it dissolve in silent awareness, choiceless awareness.

*

The breath and verticality

Without trying to make ourselves straight, the breath can bring us to verticality.

Sitting:

Visualise each inhalation coming up from the ground, up through the spine to the crown of the head (or to the back of your neck).

Visualise each exhalation from the crown of your head (or the back of your neck) upwards towards the ceiling or the sky.

Let the inhalation bring you to verticality and feel the exhalation extending it.

You can do this practice either following your natural breathing or with deep breathing.

Alternatively, visualise the breath from the ground to the level of the nostrils, the exhalation into the space in front.

After the exercise experience your effortless verticality and its impact.

*

Healing with the breath

We can use the breath to nourish and heal the body.

There may be a part of the body that feels unhealthy, diseased, painful, contracted or just a bit dead; we can direct our breath there with the help of visualisation.

Sitting or lying:

First come to the sensation of that particular area.

Now direct each in-breath towards it.

Feel an expansion of the area with each inhalation, a dissolving with each exhalation.

Let the feeling of warmth and life return to this part of the body.

You can also visualise a colour to the breath as you direct it.

When you finish, be one with this part of your body, only in the feeling.

Now let it merge in your totality.

PRANAYAMA: NADI SHODHANA

ALTERNATE NOSTRIL BREATHING

This breath stimulates the upward-flowing subtle energies in the body and brings balance and harmony to the whole system.

>Be in a comfortable sitting position.
>
>Come to the living feeling of your body, feel your globality.
>
>Feel the natural flow of the breath, feel it effortless.
>
>Feel the space of your left nostril.
>
>Feel the touch of the air.
>
>Feel the energy, the *prana* that is within the breath, like an electric wire inside its casing.
>
>Likewise with the right nostril.

Feel the different quality of the inhalation and exhalation: the temperature, the humidity.

You might find the breath more prominent in one nostril compared to the other; this is because about every two hours one nostril is more dilated than the other due to changes in the tissues in the lining of the nostrils.

Without using your fingers to control, just feel the inhalation through the left nostril, the pause, the exhalation through the right nostril and the pause. Continue: in right, out left, etc. Do several rounds.

Now we use the fingers to control in the traditional manner. Make a fist with your right hand (or the left hand could be used instead), open your ring and little fingers, open your thumb, place the ring finger to the side of the left nostril, your thumb by the side of your right nostril.

Closing your right nostril, breathe in through the left nostril. Now, closing the left nostril, breathe out through the right. Continue: breathe in right, breathe out left.

Keep your head straight and don't use more pressure than is necessary to close the individual nostril; it should feel very light.

Be sure you don't lift your right shoulder, otherwise you will soon get tense; your elbow should be pointing straight down. Also, be careful that your shoulders don't rise up with the inhalation.

Go to the end with the exhalation, but without the slightest strain.

At the end of the exhalation still have the impression that your out-breath continues in a subtle form.

Wait for the need to breathe in.

Without strain, use your whole capacity to inhale. Feel your expansion at the end of the inhale, wait in it, make it an offering to the space around you, then exhale. Feel the stream of air—like playing a flute.

You're one with the breathing, there is no thinking.

Go with the flow of your breath, don't impose artificial ratios on the length of the inhale, exhale and pause, otherwise there is violence to the mechanism.

You must discover your own capacity.

Keep the spaciousness of your mouth, and your jaw and tongue relaxed.

To avoid contraction remind yourself often of the space around you until it becomes your natural habitat.

Finish with the exhale through the left nostril.

Don't control your breath any more and just for a while feel the subtlety of your breathing.

And now let go your attention to your breath, just be in non-focused attention.

Be in the moment, the moment you cannot think.

Even when we breathe out completely, we never actually empty the lungs, since there is always a residual volume.

*

Other sequences:

Breathe in through both nostrils, exhale left,
breathe in through both nostrils, exhale right.

*

What Jean called *Raja Pranayama*:

Breathe in through both nostrils, exhale through the left,
breathe in through the left nostril, exhale through the right,
breathe in through both, exhale through right,
breathe in through the right, exhale through left,
breathe in through both nostrils, exhale through left.

Some of the more advanced techniques, such as the retention of breath, the bandas, *ujjayi*, *bastrika*, or *kapalabhati*, are better learnt directly under the guidance of a teacher. Suffice to say here each stage must be carefully learnt, and only when the student is ready. Such techniques, like much else in yoga, are often taught in a mechanical way and hence are of little value. Indeed, when they are not correctly learnt, a great deal of reaction can be created, so instead of freeing the body, tensions accumulate.

*

The breath as a pointer to the ultimate

The breath can be used in two ways: firstly to slow down the mind and to direct the subtle energies in the body.

Secondly, it can have a more direct spiritual purpose, when we emphasise the space and the silence between each breath. Here the breath is a pointer to the ultimate; we are in identity with the timeless.

EXPANDING IN THE SPACE

In a comfortable sitting position, feel where you touch the ground, feel where the weight of your body rests.

Experience your body without conceptualising it, as if you've never seen it.

Feel the different parts.

Come to the feeling of your totality.

Feel your body pervading the ground.

Feel the energy from the ground rising up through your body bringing you to verticality.

Have the temperature feeling of your body, let the warmth melt the solidity.

Let it be feeling, let it be vibration.

Come to the feeling of the front of your body, give it space to expand.

Does it really have any border?

Can you feel it totally expanded in the space in front of you?

Feel the radiation from your body covering the wall in front of you.

Sustain this feeling of openness in front of you. Really live in the space.

How does it make you feel?

Continue by doing the same with the space on your left, on your right and behind you.

Now don't emphasise any one direction, feel your globality—you're not localised anywhere.

We may call it the original body feeling, free from all psychosomatic residues.

In this feeling of spaciousness, free from living in the head, there is a fore-feeling of our real nature, a sense of freedom from all borders and limitations.

Now, don't focus any longer on this experience of expansion, for it too is an object, subtle though it may be. Let it be absorbed in silent presence; in spaceless, timeless awareness. For all that is objective is just a reminder to take us back to our homeground, that which is beyond all thought, all experience.

*

Bring space to your body

Let your body come alive as sensation.

Visualise the empty space in front of you.

Bring this empty space to fill the front of your body.

Visualise the empty space behind you.

Bring this empty space to fill the back of your body.

Visualise the empty space to your left.

Bring this empty space to fill the left side of your body.

Proceed with the right side.

Feel yourself one with the space around you.

In normal localisation there's a constant stimulation to think. In the global feeling the energy is no longer striking the forebrain, the mind becomes quiet and we are free from ourselves.

*

Bring space to your joints

Through tension we tend to pull inwards into the joints, creating fixation and rigidity in our limbs and movements. This exercise is to free the joints of their contraction.

> Lying on the floor, or perhaps sitting:
>
> Feel your contact with the ground and feel the giving of the weight.
>
> Feel your wrists; and now visualise empty space and bring this empty space to fill your wrists.
>
> Stay with this feeling of emptiness in your wrists and feel how it begins to affect them and the adjoining areas.
>
> Do the same with the elbows and shoulders.
>
> You can do the same with the joints of your fingers.
>
> Now feel the effect on the whole of your arms.
>
> Can you feel the bones floating between the joints?
>
> Now proceed with the joints of your ankles, visualise empty space and bring this space to fill your ankles.

Feel how it affects this area.

Continue with the knees and hips and feel how the whole of the legs are affected.

You will need to remind yourself often of this new sense of space until the old habits of contraction and defence disappear and this new feeling becomes natural to you.

*

Letting your bones float away

Lying (this can be adapted for sitting):

Come to the feeling of space in the joints of your fingers and visualise each bone floating away from the joint.

You'll feel your fingers becoming longer.

From the feeling of space in your wrists feel your hands floating away.

In like manner let the bones in your forearms float away from your elbows.

And the bones in your upper arms float away from your shoulders.

From the feeling of space in your ankles let the feet float away.

Now let the bones in your lower legs float away from your knees.

And the bones in the upper legs float away from your hips.

Feel space at the top of your spine, and let your head float freely away.

Feel space at the base of your spine and let the pelvis float freely away.

Feel space between your vertebrae and let them unravel themselves.

How does this affect you physically, psychologically?

*

From one healthy part: letting the feeling spread

Sitting or lying:

Let your body come alive, let it be sensation.

Note all the different sensations that make up the body.

Let your awareness rest in one particular area that feels

comfortable, relaxed and spacious.

Welcome the sensation in this part of the body, stay with it, let it deepen and unfold.

The sensation may begin to expand by itself, but we can also use visualisation to encourage it to encompass the adjoining areas.

Slowly, with the help of visualisation, let this sense of space and aliveness spread throughout your body.

You may encounter areas that are frozen, resistant to this feeling; don't be stuck here, just ignore them, go around them and continue to the extremities. Once you come to the global feeling these areas of resistance will also begin to dissipate.

Feel your whole body participate in this aliveness, and feel the expansion in space.

FROM BEING TO SENSATION TO MOVEMENT

If we have first understood, or have the deep conviction, that in our real nature there is nothing to become, nothing to attain, then we can explore the body and its movements without end-gaining. We can practise yoga to free us from what we are not, and perhaps more profoundly, simply for the joy of it.

We have looked at the importance of first experiencing the body as sensation and giving it time to reveal itself as vibration, as subtle energy, as space. Otherwise, exercising a contracted body and only working on the muscular level merely reinforces the existing patterns. This is why there are people who have practised yoga for many years and who may have become more flexible or stronger, but are still full of contraction and defence.

> *When we emphasise the feeling sensation, we use our muscles in a different way. Our muscle is in antagonistic function. This means that in this movement there is an agonist and antagonist. In other words, there is one part of the muscle which contracts and the other which expands. When the muscle is wrongly used, there is an*

over-contraction and an over-stretching, but when we use our muscles with aware feeling, these over-activities are reduced and the muscles, in a certain way, come together and function harmoniously.

Jean Klein, *Living Truth*

Jean Klein taught the *asanas* and *pranayama* that belong to yoga and called his approach Yoga in the Kashmir Tradition or just 'body work'. He had some ambivalence about the word yoga to describe what he taught because so much of yoga is taught only on the musculoskeletal level, a glorified gymnastics with little to do with the harmonisation of body and mind and the awakening of the subtle energies.

Jean also had reservations about certain dualistic tendencies in yoga: yoga means to join, but to join what? We are one from the beginning; we only have to see it. The emphasis here is not on achieving something but on listening and exploring without will or effort. In the progressive approach one evolves through various levels of spiritual attainment. But there is always a someone, an ego, still evolving. In the direct approach there is simply recognising the false as false, that you can never be something objective. The personal has no role to play.

Although Jean had trained as a medical doctor, his teaching of the yoga *asanas* did not stress the anatomical detail of positioning of bones or lengthening particular muscles. Instead, what was emphasised was first exploring the body as sensation and coming to the original expanded body. From this freedom the *asana* is explored. We avoid all anticipation, which would mean that we are already in the future, end-gaining, in an idea, rather than in the sensation of the moment. The correct position is not something imposed from the mind, but grows organically from the inner feeling. There is no dominance or violence towards the body, which is often the case in the way yoga is taught. The posture, may well look correct and properly aligned from the outside, but unless there is an inner understanding and sensitivity it is incorrect, a mere facade.

From this quality of feeling, one of spaciousness, we are asked, for instance, to feel ourselves covering the wall in front, not to manipulate certain muscles. The body is trusted to find its own release and openings and not to be imposed upon by a controller. We are asked to feel the integration of the posture, feel our oneness with space and not to live in the head department.

Certain yoga *asanas* can be said to be archetypes; that is they bring about the harmonisation of the energies of the whole body-mind. Of course, if the body is not prepared, alive as sensation, felt as space, the *asana* has little meaning.

There is a joy in feeling the elasticity of the body and discovering movement free as a wild animal on the Savanna. The practice is a celebration of existence.

In the following pages we will take some examples of movement and yoga *asanas* and how we would approach them. The principles thereof can be transposed to all postures, or indeed to life in general.

*

Raising arms

By first discovering empty, fluid movements in our arms it will then be easier to transpose this quality to more complex movements.

> Let us begin lying on the ground (the instructions can be adapted to sitting or standing):
>
> Allow yourself to relax into the floor.
>
> Feel where the weight of your body meets the ground; feel each part and the whole; do you really give the weight to the ground?
>
> Once we release the weight, along with the tension and holding, we can begin to explore the body as sensation. Follow the same instruction as in 'Letting the Sensation Unfold' (p.23). Wait for the sensation to appear, don't be in a hurry, let it come to you. All parts of the body are sensitive if we allow them to be.
>
> Now focus on the feeling of your hands and arms; be one with the sensation, don't imprison it in memory, in a concept.
>
> From the feeling raise your right arm to the vertical.

You're one with the sensation moment to moment – there's no thinking.
It may help you to keep your eyes closed so there is no distraction—you are only in the feeling.

Stretch the feeling of your arm, feel its elasticity.

Now come back; can you feel the density of the air as you lower the arm?

What is the quality of the feeling during the movement?

Does your arm feel light or heavy, dense or spacious?

Do you feel any reactions as you go through the movements or can you keep the same feeling?

Now proceed with the left arm.

Is the feeling any different to the right?

You can do these movements several times; discover a fluidity, an emptiness in your movements. Don't be caught up on the muscular level.

Take note of how your arms feel after the movements.

*

In the standing position:

Feel your contact with the ground.

How does the ground feel: hard, soft, warm, cool? What is its texture?

Just let your feet inform you.

Is the weight equally balanced between each foot and over the soles of your feet?

How are your arms?

Feel them falling towards the ground.

Is there any tendency to raise your shoulders?

Is your belly relaxed?

Feel the weight go in the ground and the energy from the ground come up through your feet, legs, hips, trunk and up through your head.

Welcome the feeling of your whole body, and feel its expansion in space.

Now from the feeling lift your right arm horizontally to the wall in front of you.

Feel it like a stream of energy going into the distance, touch the wall in front of you.

Take your arm to the vertical, touch the ceiling.

Have you collected any parasites, reactions during your movement, or does the feeling stay empty, homogeneous?

Take your arm to the side, touch the wall and return.

How does your arm feel after the movement?

Compare this arm with the other arm.

Whilst you move your arm can you feel it as a movement within your whole body?

Proceed with the left arm, making the same movements.

And now with both arms.

Although these are very simple movements, to accomplish them correctly may take some time if there are deep-seated tensions held in the arms and shoulders. You can find many variations that can be explored in these arm movements.

WORKING WITH THE ENERGY BODY

The energy body surrounds and permeates the physical body; it gives it life.

It is of a more subtle nature than the physical part. In its radiation it permeates the space around us so that we feel ourselves completely expanded in space without centre or periphery. Jean sometimes spoke about how when we walk into a dark room, it's because of the sensitivity of our energy body that we are able to avoid knocking against objects.

However, as mentioned before, this energy feeling is generally paralysed due to neuro-muscular tension. When it awakens, it eats up the feeling of solidity. It is the healing factor in the body.

The yoga postures can first be carried out moving only this energetic part, while the physical part remains still. We then repeat the posture incorporating the physical part.

Working with the energy body helps to free us of fixed patterns and memory so that when we bring in the physical part it has a greater freedom.

At first, accomplishing the posture with the energetic body may feel more like a visualisation; later we feel the energy move as it is directed.

Working with the energetic body has its own effect so, if we can't carry out the postures physically, we can do them on the energetic level and feel their benefit.

PASCHIMOTTANASANA:
SITTING FORWARD BEND

During this whole exercise it may be helpful to close your eyes so that there is no visual distraction and you stay one with the feeling.

> Sitting on the floor, the legs straight in front:
>
> Feel the contact with the ground; give the weight of your left leg, allow it to merge with the ground, and now the right leg.
>
> Feel the weight of both.
>
> To help a deeper letting go of your legs let your spine slowly sink, lumbar, dorsal and cervical in turn.
>
> Now feel a complete letting go of your legs and hips, feel them melting into the ground, or have the feeling they're sinking into soft sand.

And now, with the feeling, slowly, effortlessly, experience your spine rising to the vertical position, all the time releasing in your legs.

Do this several times, exhaling with the sinking, inhaling with the rising.

Come to the feeling of the soles of your feet, feel the warmth and radiation spreading in front, now cover the wall with this feeling.

We will first carry out the posture with the energy body, the invisible body, without moving the physical part.

Have the whole feeling of your body.

Feel the space around you.

Feel the front of your body.

Keeping the feeling alive, go out in the space in front of you and have the feeling of your energy body covering your legs.

Give all your energy to the posture, but be sure there is not the slightest movement in the physical part.

Hold this for a while.

Now come back slowly and feel the integration with the physical part.

Now take the physical part with you, but keep alive this energetic body.

The legs can be straight, if that is comfortable, or otherwise the knees can be slightly bent.

It is important that you give your own order from your inner feeling and do not just react to the instruction of a teacher.

Be free from anticipation and live moment to moment in the sensation.

You can't feel and think at the same time.

When we live moment-to-moment in the sensation, without thought, each time we do the posture it is fresh, it feels as if we are doing it for the first time. We are not living in memory, in repetition, but in the timeless.

In this approach there is nothing to achieve and no goal that is not already realised.

There is no doer, only doing, no breather, only breathing, no one who lives, only life.

Be sure there is no reaction in your movement; the moment you feel a reaction, a contraction, come back a little, or completely, and let your body be more deeply sensed. Then, with this extra sensitivity explore the posture again.

Place your hands on the ground either side of the feet, give the weight of the hands to the ground, feel the weight of your arms, your shoulders and upper back all falling into your hands.

The hands are not used to grasp the feet and pull us into the posture, rather we go deeper into the posture by releasing.

In this posture you're not trying to get your head to your knees, which would only curve the back, but rather to emphasise the flexion from the hips so that the whole spine can lengthen out along the legs.

From the outside, the chest looks enclosed, but when we live with the sensation it's completely open.

Now, with the feeling, lift the right arm parallel with the ground and touch the distance, then place the hand on the ground again.

Repeat with the left arm and then with both arms at the same time.

Feel the elongation of the whole upper body.

In the posture feel the natural flow of your breath, feel it alive in different parts.

Now go knowingly into your breathing and expand it, go to the end with the exhalation, fill the whole lungs with the inhalation. Respect the spaces, the empty moments, between each breath.

Your own body will tell you how long to hold the posture, but it needs a certain time to experience the full effect of any posture.

Now that you've experienced the integration of the whole posture and its oneness with space, don't emphasise any more what you feel—the body, the sensation. Don't lose yourself in the body, rather let the body lose itself in you, in awareness. Otherwise we are stuck in subject to object relationship. The body, the sensation, comes from awareness. When the sensation has completely unfolded, in other words released itself, let it also die in awareness. Rest in silence, choiceless presence.

Coming out of the posture keep the sensation alive.

Feel your new body; don't go back to the old pattern.

Feel how the posture affects you; stay with this new feeling, don't rush on to the next posture. The effect of the posture is after the posture when a re-orchestration of energy takes place.

Often we go back to an old pattern to give us security and familiarity with the known, instead of staying with the new feeling of expansion that is experienced after a well-executed posture.

*

Here are some suggestions that can be used on occasion in the posture:

Perhaps there is part of your body that feels resistant: direct your breathing to that particular part. Feel how it affects it.

*

Visualise warm hands resting on your lumbar back, feel the warmth going into the back; do the same in the dorsal and shoulder areas.

*

Feel your whole back and visualise it falling into your front; feel the front of your body, the chest and abdomen, and visualise it falling into the ground.

*

Visualise the space in front of the chest and breathe in this space; now have the feeling you're breathing in the space beneath the floor.

*

Feel in turn the expansion of your front, the left side, the right side, the back and then as one expansion.

Working with the *asana* is a pretext to come to our original nature. The body is an expression of awareness, of consciousness, and ultimately nothing but consciousness.

We allow all perceptions to come back to their home ground. When understood in this light, all is made sacred; the world and every so-called object, for there is nothing apart from this ultimate reality. The body is glorified as is every speck of dust.

ARDHA MATSYENDRASANA:
HALF SPINAL TWIST

Sitting with the legs straight in front, bend the left leg across the front of the body and place the right foot over the left knee. If possible keep both sit bones in contact with the ground.

Feel your contact with the ground and allow your verticality to arise from here.

Feel the different parts of your body: the legs, hips, trunk, hands, arms, shoulders and head. And now come to the feeling of the whole.

From this wholeness feel your expansion in space.

Let the feeling dissolve the solidity; you are one with space.

Keeping alive this energetic quality, turn to the right with your energy body; hold this for a while.

Now come back and collect the physical part, feel the integration, and this time bring it with you. As you turn to the right wrap your left arm around the right thigh, with your right hand resting on the floor behind you.

Feel yourself turning round a central axis, all the while keeping your verticality.

Try not to lean backwards. It is the spine that keeps you straight, so try to avoid pushing with your right hand; it just rests on the floor.

As you move into the posture can you do so without creating reactions, keeping the empty feeling of your body?

Are you aware of the space around you or has your attention got lost in the musculoskeletal structure of your body?

As soon as you lose the space feeling there is invariably contraction and the old patterns return.

As you keep the posture, turn your head in the opposite direction.

Can you turn your head independently without the slightest movement of your shoulders or trunk?

This notion of independent movement is an important element in the freedom of the body. Often when we make a movement with one part of the body, other parts are in reaction. For example, when raising the right arm to the vertical, we may find ourselves unconsciously lifting the left shoulder.

> Now feel the double direction, emphasise both.
>
> Now again turn your head to the right; how far do you see?
>
> Feel the integration of the posture.
>
> Can you feel it as one with the space around you?
>
> Only be still; there's nothing to think.
>
> After the appropriate time come back and repeat with the other side.
>
> Afterwards feel the effect of the posture.
>
> You could also do a forward bend between changing from one side to the other.

TRIKONASANA: TRIANGLE

> Standing with your feet about a metre apart, turn to the right, your right foot turning out 90 degrees and your left foot angled inwards. Your chest faces the right leg.

> Feel your feet anchored in the ground, feel the ground in your feet.

Jean would on occasion, much to the amusement of all, jump into the air and land with a thud to remind us to really feel the ground.

> Feel your whole posture and your chest open, and now go out into the space and cover the right leg (bend the right knee a little if you feel strained).

> Place the right hand on the inside of the right leg with the palm open and the left hand on the left hip.

> Turn your hips to the front, followed by the chest and

then the head. Then take your left hand to the vertical and look upwards.

Feel your whole body open to the space in front of you.

Feel the expansion of your arms, feel their alignment from fingertips to fingertips—it's one line.

Feel your spine as one line, and the head as a continuation of the spine.

If you feel some tension in the left arm, place your hand again on your hip, and now raise it, but this time really keep the feeling, the lightness.

Heaviness and density may be there because we have still not let the deeper sensation of our body unfold.

How is your neck? If there is some discomfort, turn your head to look downwards and then, with the feeling, turn it again to look up without becoming fixated.

Feel how you breathe; take note that often when there is some tension we inhibit the breathing, thereby accentuating the tension.

Feel your whole body as an expression in space, without borders. Live in this space.

Again cover the right leg and now swivel into the centre, the feet facing forward, and come up in a straight line, imagining you're a puppet being drawn up from the crown of your head.

Proceed with the posture on the other side.

After the posture return to the standing pose—*tadasana*—and feel the vibration of your body.

The breath, as we have seen earlier, can be used in many ways. Jean would often encourage deep breathing in a posture when it was appropriate, especially in the sitting forward bends. Deep breathing can give more power to the postures. At other times the breathing is allowed to follow its own course, letting the breath breathe you.

There is not one approach to each posture, there are many variations and possibilities to experiment with; this keeps the practice fresh. We might, for example, begin *trikonasana* with the arms out to the horizontal and then proceed into the pose, or combine *trikonasana* with *parivrtta trikonasana* (reverse triangle).

*

Some further suggestions to be used on occasion in *trikonasana*:

Deepen your breathing and with each inhalation expand the posture, feel all directions, give a little with each exhalation.

So work with the in–breath, give a little with the out-breath.

*

Visualise the posture three metres in front of you. Now with your energy body occupy that space, give it all your energy. Come back, take note how the posture feels now.

*

Feel your whole posture, offer it to the space around you.

*

Feel your whole posture as breath, feel it as an inhalation, feel it as an exhalation.

When you become more sensitive to your body
you have the impression that
the inhalation-exhalation is no longer localised.
It is all around you.
It is important to see how we live mainly in our heads.
Think with your whole body,
feel with your whole body.
In the whole feeling, the global sensation,
you go into your room and touch your whole room.
You go outside and touch the clouds, the trees, the water.
You do not live in isolation.
In your radiation you are in communion with all things.
In this expansion there is no place for the ego
because the ego is a contraction.
Love is expansion, a feeling of spaciousness.

Jean Klein, *The Ease of Being*

MEDITATION

Most forms of meditation are in subject-object relationship: there is a focus of attention, a concentration on something, be it the breath, the body, a sound or image. And whilst it is true that such practices help to slow down the activities of the mind, the practitioner is maintaining the dualism of observer and something observed. Invariably, once the mind is no longer tethered to its particular focus, the mind with all its vagaries soon rushes back to reclaim its usual territory. A controlled mind, through any technique, is hardly a free mind.

We can talk about meditation as a practice, but meditation in its deepest meaning is to rest in our real nature, to be what we are—knowingly. It is not a cerebral activity or even a non-activity, it's beyond all opposites.

We don't know ourselves in silence, but only through a collection of images, thoughts and feelings. It is the continuous mind-chatter and daydreaming that keep alive this self-image. This chatter and daydreaming, which we may hardly be aware of, are a defence, a fear of being nobody. The natural function of the mind is movement; this is not a problem except when this movement revolves around an illusory personal entity. This entity finds it difficult to be free of intention and to sit in silence without some technique. We may feel bored, or overwhelmed by a ceaseless train of thought, or disturbed by fears and emotions we thought were long since dealt with. We find it difficult to face ourselves, and accept what arises moment to moment.

However, it is only through a disinterested welcoming, an acceptance of what is, that there can be any real transformation. Acceptance here is nothing to do with passive resignation to a situation but is more like a scientist seeing facts as they are. This is not psychological acceptance, where the ego feels a surrender, but an active functional acceptance of facts.

In this welcoming, which is without judgment, comparison, resistance or hidden motive, we are no longer an accomplice to the situation, no longer fuelling the problem. Since the ego is no longer centre stage, we find ourselves outside the drama. There is a picture show going on, but it's not ours and there is no need to do anything with it. There arises spontaneously a space relationship between what is observed and the observing. The show is in me, but I'm not in the show. When there is complete acceptance, the accepted dies in the accepting. When there is no longer any emphasis on the objective part, when we look for nothing from the object, we find ourselves in accepting, in openness. There is a glimpse of freedom, of autonomy from what we took ourselves to be.

As we touched on before, it is difficult to come to a quiet mind when the body is a field of contraction, resistance and defence and the breathing dominated by fear. So first face the body: a relaxed body is already the beginning of a relaxed mind.

What we experience as the body is largely a superimposition of density veiling the primal body. Once the layers of density in the body are allowed to dissolve, it is found to be open, transparent, one with space. The breathing is allowed to be free of somebody doing the breathing.

In ordinary localisation, where there is the impression that we live in a body, and more particularly in the head, there is a constant stimulation to think. In exploring the body we come to the expanded body, the global feeling. In this feeling of non-localisation we are free from the head and the constant mind-chatter. The body is in my awareness but my awareness is no longer limited to the body.

In exploring the body we let the body express its true nature, its transparency. Once the body is relieved of its borders, its density, it dissolves back into awareness.

Even with the sense of a light, expanded body, thought patterns don't cease to exist. However, they are likely to slow down and we may begin to notice space between thoughts—empty moments.

Meditation may be said to be both active and passive. Active in the sense there is the natural alertness of the body-mind, passive in that there is no projection of some result, no end-gaining.

Meditation is not doing something, rather it is choiceless awareness. It is not an introversion of the senses; trying to stop the senses functioning is violence. So we let what wants to arise, arise and let each thought dissolve like a bubble coming up from the depth of the ocean. There is no need to analyse or follow each thought. If we do so, we keep the thought alive, we fuel it. After a while we learn, without violence, to ignore the thought.

> *If you take a bite of a rotten apple you don't need to eat the whole apple to prove it.*
>
> Jean Klein

Ask yourself what is the origin of a thought and who is the thinker of such a thought? Explore to find out if there really is such an entity. You will discover there is no such entity, only a silence that is beyond the mind to fathom.

This direct approach to meditation may not be for everyone. It is usually helpful, when we start meditation, to focus our attention on something to avoid being overwhelmed by thought. The breath is like a natural mantra, and perhaps the easiest to focus on. However we should realise this is a kind of crutch and we should be ready to drop it when we no longer need it and not become dependent on any technique.

We may start a meditation practice with the focus on some object. Over time, this may become more and more subtle until we arrive at its least substantial form. However, this still remains a subtle object outside ourselves; we remain in subject-object relationship. Since we have always emphasised the object part and ignored the ultimate subject, self-knowledge remains an enigma.

In choiceless awareness we do not emphasise what comes

and goes in awareness, but awareness itself. But don't try to be aware, you are awareness in any case. When we have a glimpse of our real nature we lose our addiction to the world of objects, we know them for what they are—simply mind. When we understand this, there is a complete letting go of striving. We feel our real nature to be this awareness, and not a body-mind. We feel our thoughts, feelings and the world are within awareness, and ultimately nothing other than awareness.

> *When you look at an object, turn your head and see the source of looking. Be aware that you are the light of all perception.*
>
> Jean Klein, *Who Am I?*

From first being identified with a perception, the body-mind, and being lost in it, we stand back from this involvement by feeling we are the witness of all that is perceived, the body-mind-world. We can talk about the witness when we make a division between the knower and the known. By taking this stance as witness there comes a sense of space, of distancing from what is observed; we feel our independence. Don't try to be the witness; see that you are the witness in any case.

But then, this interim device of feeling oneself to be the witness of all that is perceived is understood to be nothing but awareness, consciousness, and there is nothing apart from consciousness.

The body, mind and world are seen in their true light, not as objects but as one with consciousness. There is nothing but consciousness, there is nothing but God.

How we see reality depends upon the standpoint from which we observe it. From the standpoint of taking myself to be a body, the world appears as form. When I take myself to be the personality, the world appears in subtle form, as mind. But from the ultimate understanding that I am consciousness, then the world is nothing other than consciousness.

Just as with the body work, with the continued practice of meditation we may think that instead of agitation slowing down, we're more aware of it. It may be that in these quiet moments thoughts and feelings arise that have been buried or suppressed. Or it may be that with a quieter mind we're more aware of its activities than ever before. In either case we allow these thoughts and feelings to arise and dissolve without judgement or being lost in them. They are expressions of silence and pointers to our real nature. Meditation is not a silent mind but the Silence beyond the mind, that ever is.

Jean stressed the importance of those quiet moments in daily life when we are free of activity, or between two thoughts. When we don't ignore these occasions but let them take us, they are windows into our real nature. At the beginning, because we are so orientated to the world of objects, we see these moments as merely vacant, as absence, but truly understood, these moments are the continuous background to all perception—our eternal presence. The more we become acquainted with these moments, the more they will solicit us, draw us to the Silence. *The Self seeks the Self*; it is always soliciting us to itself.

It is also important to understand the nature of desire. When something we desire is attained there is an experience of desirelessness, and with it the feeling of happiness. We attribute this happiness to the object and come to believe that happiness resides in objects and therefore continue our quest to possess things. If we were to look deeply into our experience, we would come to see that it isn't the object that gives us happiness but rather, just for that moment we are desireless, we are at peace, no longer looking for anything. When there is happiness, there is nobody who is happy and there is no cause of the happiness. Our real desire is to be desireless.

Jean also emphasised the importance of letting go of all our holding and identification before we fall asleep at night, dying to the world of objects, and going into sleep in our nakedness. How we fall asleep at night governs how deeply we sleep and how we wake up in the morning.

When we first wake up in the morning there is still the perfume of deep sleep, before the world of objects and all our habits appear. At this moment we know we are, but we are free of all representation. This is an important moment. We should stay with this space and let the world come to life *in* our awareness. It is also at this time that sitting meditation is most appropriate, when the planet is still quiet.

A meditation practice may become part of the rhythm of our day. We may find ourselves naturally drawn to the silence. However, if we impose the practice on ourselves through will and discipline, we will end up with another rigidity rather than freedom. If we feel something lacking after missing a practice, then it has become merely a habit.

To come to a quiet mind, and ultimately to come to know ourselves, the mind must be informed, it must know its limits.

As long as we think we can grasp reality with the mind, we will continually stimulate thought. Only when we understand that reality is beyond the mind, does the mind give up. In a certain way the mind has to exhaust itself for humility to arise. We are then open to what's beyond the mind; we are open to the unknown. We live in the innocence of not-knowing. It is only in this state of openness that we are available to what is beyond the mind.

We may believe ourselves to be awareness, beyond the person, or have a deep conviction of it, but the reality still eludes us. It is not until this personal entity disappears that truth is known, that is, *being* the truth. This is an instantaneous understanding, beyond space and time.

This entity disappears when the belief that sustained it has no hold, when it is seen as pure illusion. Even so, the residues of this belief don't disappear overnight. Such residues, which are fixed energy, belong to time and space and it takes time for them to dissolve. But since they are no longer fuelled by a belief system they are dead embers in a fire and are of no concern. They cannot distract from knowing our real nature.

Jean likened meditation practice to a laboratory wherein we explore who is the meditator. When we discover there is no meditator, then we give up meditation, then meditation *is*. It becomes more and more integrated into our daily life. That is, we *are* it; it is the background of all function and non-function, our eternal presence.

When we truly understand that all that can be attained is still an object, we stop our projection and are open to the unknown. As long as we are still searching for some thing, we stay on the level of the mind. As long as there is the slightest intention in our meditation, we remain in the becoming process; it is a denial of the Self. That which is beyond time and space is not to be attained by mind or will. It comes in our not-knowing, our total innocence, our total surrender. And we truly surrender when we realise there is no one to surrender.

> *The knower can never be known, it is its own knowing… you may feel it as a current of love, but it is silence.*
>
> Jean Klein

GUIDED MEDITATION

Come to a comfortable sitting position.

Feel where you give the weight of your body.

Feel where your hands are resting.

Welcome the feeling of the whole body.

Come to the inner feeling of your verticality and the space around you.

How do you experience your face? Is there any tension? Be aware of it, let the tension come up and express itself, and let it dissolve.

Experience your eyes, first feeling the space of the orbits. And now experience the eyes, letting the sensation completely unfold.

Let the tensions you hold come up and dissolve.

Feel the eyes fill the whole space of the orbits.

Feel a deep relaxation in your eyes.

Let your eyes be like globes filling space.

Your eyes are connected to the back of your brain just above your neck by the optic nerve.

Let your awareness go backwards from your eyes to the back of your head.

Feel yourself in the back of your head.

Let the feeling expand, be in this spaciousness behind you.

Be in this quietness behind you, free of your forehead.

Stay localised in this space for a while.
See how it affects you.

Let your awareness come downward from the back of your neck to the heart centre.

Feel yourself in the heart.

Let the feeling expand.

Feel yourself in expansion.

Let the heart be light.
Be the light.

Let yourself be non-localised.

Let the silence come to you.

The silence you cannot think.

QUOTATIONS FROM *VIJNANA BHAIRAVA*

The Practice of Centering Awareness,
translated by Swami Lakshman Joo

Verse 25
Oh Bhairavi, by focusing one's awareness on the two voids (at the end) of the internal and external breath, thereby the glorious form of Bhairava is revealed through Bhairavi.

Verse 43
One should meditate on the void in one's own body on all sides simultaneously. When the mind has become free from thoughts, one experiences everything as the Void.

Verse 60
One should cast one's gaze on an open (stretch of) land devoid of trees, mountains, walls, etc. When the state of mind is fixed there, then the fluctuating thoughts dissolve (by themselves).

Verse 62
When the awareness has abandoned one object and remains fixed without moving on to another object, then through the state in between (the two) the supreme realisation will unfold.

Verse 63
If one contemplates simultaneously that one's entire body or the world consists of nothing but Consciousness, then the mind becomes free from thoughts and the supreme awakening occurs.

Verse 75
One should concentrate on the state when sleep has not yet come, but the external awareness has disappeared (between waking and sleep)—there the supreme Goddess reveals herself.

Verse 92
One should meditate on one's own Self in the form of a vast sky, unlimited in all directions, then the Power of Consciousness is free of any support and reveals her own nature.

Verse 128
Fixing one's mind on the external space which is eternal, supportless, empty, all pervading and free from limitation, in this way one will be absorbed in non-space.

Recommended Books

Books by Jean Klein:
Be who you are
I Am
Who Am I?
The Ease of Being
Transmission of the Flame
Living Truth
Beyond Knowledge
Open to the Unknown
The Book of Listening

Books by Sri Atmananda (Krishna Menon):
Notes on Spiritual Discourses
Atma Darshan
Atma Nirvriti

Yoga, Art of Relaxation, Keers, Lewensztain and Malavika
Yoga Corps de Vibration, Corps de Silence, Eric Baret
Yoga volgens de Kashmirmethode, Koos Zondervan
The Nature of Man According to the Vedanta, John Levy
Immediate Knowledge and Happiness, John Levy
Talks with Sri Ramana Maharishi
Be As You Are, The Teachings of Sri Ramana Maharshi, edited by David Godman
I Am That, Nisargadatta
Choiceless Awareness, J. Krishnamurti
Eternity Now, Francis Lucille
The Perfume of Silence, Francis Lucille

Presence, Rupert Spira
The Ashes of Love, Rupert Spira
This is Always Enough, John Astin

Also available by Billy Doyle from Non-Duality Press

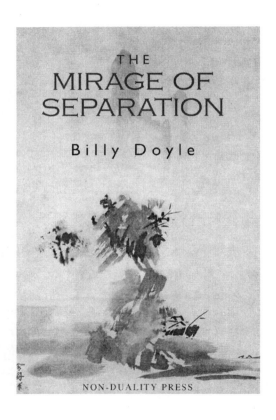

CONSCIOUS.TV is a TV channel which broadcasts on the internet at www.conscious.tv. It also has programmes shown on several satellite and cable channels around the world including the Sky system in the UK where you can watch programmes at 8.30 pm every evening on channel No. 192. The channel aims to stimulate debate, question, enquire, inform, enlighten, encourage and inspire people in the areas of Consciousness, Non-Duality and Science. It also has a section called 'Life Stories' with many fascinating interviews.

There are over 200 interviews to watch including several with communicators on Non-Duality including Richard Bates, Burgs, Billy Doyle, Bob Fergeson, Jeff Foster, Steve Ford, Suzanne Foxton, Gangaji, Greg Goode, Scott Kiloby, Richard Lang, Francis Lucille, Roger Linden, Wayne Liquorman, Jac O'Keefe, Mooji, Catherine Noyce, Tony Parsons, Halina Pytlasinska, Genpo Roshi, Satyananda, Richard Sylvester, Rupert Spira, Florian Schlosser, Mandi Solk, James Swartz, Art Ticknor, Joan Tollifson, and Pamela Wilson. There is also an interview with UG Krishnamurti. Some of these interviewees also have books available from Non-Duality Press.

Do check out the channel as we are interested in your feedback and any ideas you may have for future programmes. Email us at info@conscious.tv with your ideas or if you would like to be on our email newsletter list.

WWW.CONSCIOUS.TV

Lightning Source UK Ltd.
Milton Keynes UK
UKOW04f1322281114

242341UK00001B/114/P